BUT GOD

Shameka Hatcher

BUT GOD

Text Copyright © 2024 by Shameka Hatcher
All rights reserved. No part of this book may be reproduced, scanned, or distributed in any printed or electronic form or by any means without prior written consent of the publisher, except for brief quotes used in reviews.
Please do not participate in or encourage piracy of copyrighted materials in violation of the author's rights. Purchase only authorized editions.

ISBN: 9798321032671

Printed in the United States

Contents

Dedication	v
Introduction	5
The Beginning	7
Test One	9
The Move	11
The Church	13
Enough	15
I Told	17
Different Levels	19
Let Us Go Deeper	21
My First Love	23
It Continues	25
He Is Better	27
Making Moves	29
Still on the Run	33
Look at God	35
My Second Relationship	37
The Bullshit	39
After the Baby	41

Year Six	43
Betrayal	45
Shay Shay	47
I am TIRED	49
I Remember!	51
What the Hell	53
The Unbelief	55
The Day of the Delivery	57
A New Beginning	59
Still Attached	61
My Life Changed	63
The Turn Around	65
God is ALIVE	67
But GOD	69
GOD Did It!	71
Now Faith	73
Acknowledgments	75
About The Author	77
Contacting the Author	77

Dedication

I would like to thank God first for life, health, strength, and knowledge. I want to thank both of my parents for showing me the true meaning of being LOVED. And thanks to my parents for bringing me up in church and teaching me about God from a young age. I'm so grateful!!

BUT GOD

Introduction

When you are chosen, you will have many tests in your life from the enemy, starting from a young age **(Psalm 105:15).** The enemy will try to use people who are close to you or in different situations to control your thoughts. The enemy will try to make you lose your mind. Why is this? The enemy knows that you are chosen and does not want you to complete the assignment that God placed you on this earth to do. One thing about God, He will always intervene.

BUT GOD

Chapter 1

The Beginning

It all began at the age of six. I knew that I was different. Now that I am older, I know the word for the way I was feeling. That word is *chosen*. The year was 1989. I was a beautiful dark-skinned little girl riding in the middle of my grandmother's grey Pinto car, headed to church in Statesboro, Georgia. Compared to my small town of Claxton, Statesboro seemed like a big city through the eyes of a six-year-old. Every Sunday, my family members and I traveled to church. As we pulled up to the church, little ole me was told to sit in the middle of the pew. However, this Sunday, something happened in church that I thought everyone witnessed, only to find out later that I was the only one to see it. I looked at the faces of my cousins sitting on the left and right of me. They did not seem to notice anything different, nor did they hear anything strange. Before my eyes appeared a cross shining like the morning sun and the sound of wind chimes. It puzzled me, but I did not say anything to anyone.

It felt like a warm unknown hug at that very moment. A hug like I never felt before. I began to feel that same hug every Sunday. I loved that feeling so much. Each Sunday, I woke up early, got dressed, and became excited about going to church. But of course, soon after the excitement wore off. My

BUT GOD

grandmother's car broke down and going to church stopped. That was when my true tests began.

Chapter 2

Test One

I loved Rosey's house, but I did not know that Steven would be there and that he had his eyes on me. Steven had a thing for little, beautiful, young innocent black girls, and he wanted me. I was only six years old, and Steven was around seventeen at the time. I loved playing in the dirt with many of my other cousins, making mud pies by using sticks and grass, and making imaginary food. Boy! What a fun time we would have.

That was until one day when Steven called me inside while everyone else was playing. Of course, all the adults had left the house at that time. I went inside unaware of the awful plan of Steven. He looked me in the eyes and told me to go into the room. He then pushed me on the bed, grabbed my hands, and put them on his penis. He then proceeded to pull down my panties, and he started to rub his penis on my vagina. He whispered in my ear, "Do not tell anyone." At that very moment, I felt the same love that I felt at the church in Statesboro. That feeling took my mind off what was happening to me, and it lasted as if the molestation wasn't happening. After Steven finished his business, I sat down with my cousins to play. Steven was looking at me, and he said with his mouth, "DON'T SAY A WORD." Of course, I did not say a word.

BUT GOD

The molestation continued over the course of two months. Every time Steven molested me, that same feeling of love from church would return. It eventually got to the point that my vagina started to burn uncontrollably. Each time I went to the bathroom, I screamed while holding my own mouth. But one day, I had to say something. The pain was unbearable. I reached out to my grandmother Mary and Aunt Susie, and I told them that my private area was hurting. I did not tell them what Steven was doing to me. They took me to a room and laid me on the bed. They instructed me to open my legs, and they rubbed Vaseline on my private area. They then asked the question, "Has someone been touching you?" I told them, "Yes, Steven."

They proceeded to tell me not to tell my mother or my father. Even as a child, I was confused. They would rather protect the monster, Steven, than an innocent child.

As time passes, I wanted to tell my parents, but I remembered the adults told me not to tell them. Instead of me telling what Steven had done to my preciously innocent body, I told my parents that Rosey was extremely mean to me. I told my mom I did not want to go to her home anymore. I was so happy when they said I no longer had to visit Rosey ever again. Then, my mom and dad moved to another area. I was so happy. I returned to being a normal child who loved playing again.

Chapter 3

The Move

The new move was good for me. I met two new friends, and I was in class with them at school. One of my friend's name was Samantha. As time passed, Samantha asked if I could spend the night with her. Of course, my mom said, "Yes." I was extremely happy. Samantha's mother and father were having a big party. It was getting extremely late, so we were told to take a bath and go to bed. Samantha's bedroom was across from the bathroom. The room light was off, but her bathroom light was on. I could see a dark figure crawling on the floor. Samantha had bunk beds, and I was on the bottom bunk. I smelled liquor on the breath of the horrible figure. The figure got in the bed behind me and started putting his fingers in my panties. The feeling from church came again and a voice said, "RUN HOME."

Running home is exactly what I did. I ran home at four o'clock in the morning and knocked hard on the door. My mom answered the door in a panic and said, "Why are you here at 4:00 a.m.?" I said "Mommy, I am scared." I wanted to tell her, but I remembered from the first test I was told not to tell.

The next morning, Samantha came to my home and asked me why I left. She said, "I know why you left. He touches

BUT GOD

me too, all the time." Of course, she looked at me and said, "Don't tell."

Chapter 4

The Church

Every summer, all the children in the community went to Vacation Bible School at a church in our town. I loved to go because we always played games, ate good soul food, and of course, learned about the Bible. One Saturday night, we had movie night. I was so excited. For the little girl's class, it was a female teacher. For the little boys' class, it was a male teacher. Before the movie started, Ms. Bertha turned the lights off in the sanctuary. I was sitting on the bleachers in front of an adult teacher, Mr. Lamar. He asked me to come sit next to him. I was only eight years old. This man placed his hand on my lap. In my mind, I was thinking there was no way Mr. Lamar would do this to me in church in front of all these people. I was wrong. Mr. Lamar went into my panties with his large hands and placed his fingers inside my private parts. In my mind, I could not believe he did this in God's church, but I was so shocked. I could not say anything. As I turned to look at him, he was looking straight ahead at the television while he was fingering me.

 The warm familiar feeling from the early church experience came back as it did many times before. The feeling stayed with me the entire time. As soon as Mr. Lamar finished fingering me, the feeling left immediately as if nothing happened. At this point, anger began to set in. I was mad at

BUT GOD

every man that I saw. Mr. Lamar also worked at the school. He said, "I have a surprise for you at school on Monday morning. Do not tell anyone what I did to you."

Monday came, and there was a huge event. The school auditorium was filled with students. Guess what Mr. Lamar did? That nasty bastard did his best to pull my name out of a box for a drawing, and I won a teddy bear, tee shirt, a trophy, and a gold necklace. I had to walk on stage in front of the whole school. You would think I would be happy, but I was angry. I had to walk in front of the whole school and smile. I had to shake this same nasty hand knowing what he had used it to do to me in church. I wanted to get the microphone and tell everyone what he did to me right then, that he just had his hands in my pussy in church two days before. I was thinking there is no telling how many other kids he touched using the organization and the church, just to get close to kids to please his sick ways.

A week later, I was in the car with my dad. Mr. Lamar was a police officer, and he pulled my daddy over. As I saw him walk towards the car, I started kicking the dashboard. Daddy said, "What is wrong with you girl? I am not going to jail." Daddy did not know, but my eyes were locked on Mr. Lamar's gun. I wanted to kill Mr. Lamar. From that day on, I stopped going to church at Mt. Pleasant, and I blocked him out of my mind forever. Or so I thought.

Chapter 5

Enough

My momma started working the night shift from 11:00 p.m. to 7:00 a.m. My sister and I had to stay with my aunt Lisa and her boyfriend Tommy. Tommy was nice to us all the time but was extremely nice to my sister. As time passed, my mom, father, and other family members noticed that my sister's body was getting wider. My mother would say my sister's chest was getting bigger, not knowing what had been going on. They thought she was maturing quickly. So, that was another test.

Late one night, my aunt went out somewhere, and my sister and I were asleep. Suddenly, my sister woke me up. My sister told me to look in the kitchen, pour all the dish liquid out of the bottle and put hot water in it. I did exactly that. She told me to hide behind the door and when Tommy entered the room to spray the hot water on his private part. All I can remember is him walking in with no clothes on and his hard penis walking towards her. I jumped from behind the door and sprayed the hot water directly on his penis. I will never forget. He grabbed his penis, hollering and backing out of the room. He was pointing at me and yelling, "I am going to get you." All my sister could do was say, "Thank you, sister." We held each other until the sun came up. She looked me in my eyes and said, "Do not tell, because if Daddy and Momma find out, they will kill Tommy. We will not see them again for a long time. Pinky promise me." I did just that.

Chapter 6

I Told

As months passed, I decided to ask my mom and dad if I could spend the night with my other friend, Stacy. She lived across the hall from our apartment. Of course, they said, "Yes." I was so happy. Stacy's mom took us to the movies and to eat pizza. We had a wonderful time. It was time to return home and settle down for the evening. Her mom said, "It's time to take a bath and get ready for bed." I did not know that her mother worked the night shift. As her mom was walking out of the door for work, her mother's boyfriend was walking in from work. As soon as my friend saw her mom's boyfriend's face, her smile turned into a frown. He told us to go to bed. About an hour later, I heard a deep voice call her name. She looked me in the eye and said, "I am about to get raped."

At that very moment, I put in my heart that I was going to tell someone. I was so angry to see my friend like that. I ran home and told my mother. My mother jumped off the couch, put her shoes on, and ran across the hall. She was knocking hard on the front door. He came to the door and my mother told him to let my friend out of the house right then. He asked "Why?" My mother told him, "The police are on the way." When the police arrived, they asked Stacy, "Where is your mother?" At that time, my mother told the police she would answer their questions.

BUT GOD

The police proceeded to question Stacy in front of my mother. She told the police that her mother's boyfriend, Stephen, had been raping her every time her mother went to work. The police knocked on the door and questioned him about the situation. Of course, he lied. But my friend kept a bag with all her bloody panties, and they took her panties and did a DNA sample. They found his DNA sample and Stephen went to jail.

I finally felt at peace knowing that I did not keep my mouth closed. This time when someone said, "Do not tell," I had the courage to tell. I found my voice. Once you learn that you have a voice, never be afraid to use it.

Chapter 7

Different Levels

At the age of twelve, my family moved to another location in town. Because of my experiences, I acted a little older and understood different things. My mother always talked to me about everything. It was a very chilly night. I would always stay up until she returned home. My dad worked at night. My grandmother babysat us until my mom arrived home. This night was different. As soon as my mom opened the door, I was happy. She would always give me hugs and kisses. This time, she went into the bathroom and stayed there for a long time. I decided to get up and check on her. The door was not locked. I walked in. She was standing up facing the tub.

  I called her name and when she turned around all I could see was blood coming from her nose. The blood would not stop. She sat me down on the floor and said "Meka, I am going to tell you the truth. I want you to know to never do this." Momma told me she tried cocaine for the first time. She said she would never do it again and told me not to let anyone in this world influence me to do so. It was so sad seeing my mom that way. From that night on, she never tried cocaine again. Each time she came in the door, I looked at her nose to make sure it was not bleeding. The scene from before always replayed in my head.

BUT GOD

One night, Momma came in and sat beside my bed. She said, "Meka, you are chosen." She covered me up with my covers, and I went to sleep.

Months passed and I was laying in my bed. All of a sudden, the warm feeling from the cross of the early church returned. This time, I saw a reflection of it on my room door. I could not move. Then I heard a voice saying, "Fret not; I am here with you." Then it went away.

As time passed, I never mentioned anything about the experience. One day, I took a nap after school. I had a dream about my mother. In the dream, she did something that really made me mad. I jumped up and told her what I dreamed about her. She ignored me. She kept looking at the television like she had never heard me. Later that night, she came to me and said, "Meka, how did you know that?" I had forgotten that I told her earlier I had a dream about her. My mother said, "Meka you are gifted, because what you dreamed, I said I would take with me to my grave."

The dreams started to come more often about different people close to me or random things that would occur. It began to scare me. I could hear the voice say, "Fret not; I am with you." My grandmother was a pastor. I told her about the dreams. She explained to me that my gift was from God, and it was okay. She said be mindful not to share with people. I just accepted my gift. I began to realize that God took me to another level because I was older, and I had finally found my voice.

Chapter 8

Let Us Go Deeper

My mom always worked the graveyard shift. She had Ms. Rosey watch us while she worked. Ms. Rosey and I had a great relationship. One night, Ms. Rosey called me out of my room and sat me at the table. She shared her life story with me. Now that I am older, I realized she was evaluating me to see if she could trust me. Ms. Rosey was paralyzed on her right side. She needed extra help around the house, and I was the one who would always help her. It was in the late 1990's, and Ms. Rosey woke me up out of my sleep and asked me to put in a VCR tape and then go back to bed. When the tape was finished, she asked me to take it out. Ms. Rosey would do this two or three times per week.

One night, I saw she was watching a porn video with two ladies having sex. One night she caught me and asked me not to tell anyone she was watching two women. After that, I never told. That let her know that she could trust me. Another night came, she asked me to get up. She handed me a twenty-dollar bill and I went outside to give it to a guy standing outside. The guy then handed me something. At the time, I did not know what it was. Now that I am older, I now know it was twenty dollars' worth of crack cocaine. I went back into the house and gave it to her. She sent me to look in the trash can

BUT GOD

for a Coke can. I could not find one. She told me to go outside to find one, so I did.

We were sitting at the kitchen table. She asked me to bring her an ash tray to the table. She had a sharp object in her pocket. At that moment, I heard God say again, "Fear not I am with you." Ms. Rosey had me fold the can up, take the ashes out of the ashtray, sit them in the middle of the can where the holes were, and she proceeded to take the crack out and sit it on top of the ashes. I was thinking I was helping her. She gave me the lighter, told me to hold the can up and put the fire on the crack. Once I put the fire on the crack, it began to sizzle. She got in a rage. She got angry. She said, "Take your ASS back to bed. You done burned up my crack."

Chapter 9

My First Love

As the older people would say, at fifteen years old, I started smelling myself. In other words, my body was developing, and I was ready to have sex. I began to disobey my parents and started skipping school. I ran into a drug dealer who introduced me to smoking weed. After my first joint, boy did I feel so good. I decided that smoking weed was what I wanted to do. I was disobeying my parents and skipping school so badly that my mom took me to the police station. I ended up on probation for being an unruly minor.

As soon as I got off probation, I turned sixteen years old. I dropped out of high school, and I began to run the streets all the time. I fell hard in love with a guy, Jo, who was about two years older than me. He had his own place, money, car, and of course, weed that I loved to smoke. Eight months later, I was pregnant. I was sixteen when I got pregnant, but I was seventeen when I had my son.

When my mom and dad found out I was pregnant, they gave me permission to leave. After the baby was born, everything was great the first year. Until one day, Jo got jealous and punched me in the face. At that point, all I could think about was how did I let my guard down. He had no clue how much I hated men because of my past experiences. Hell took over me! I told myself I would be ready for him if he ever laid a hand on me again!

One day I decided when he came home, I would jump on him. When he walked through the door, I hit him over the head with a glass vase. As soon as I saw the blood, it made me feel good to see a man hurt. I know that may sound crazy to some, but it really made me feel good based on my past experiences. As time passed, the fights became regular. My son went to stay with his grandmother. It got to the point, that I wanted to kill Jo. I gathered everything in the house that was glass and broke it.

My dad walked into the house and asked me what was going on. I told him that Jo and I were fighting. My dad and Jo had words, and they started to fight. When I saw Jo fighting my dad, I felt heat rising from my body. I was so angry. Good thing my daddy said, "Meka, get you stuff and let's go." I left with my daddy. Jo kept begging me to come back. A month and a half later, I gave in and returned.

Chapter 10

It Continued

Jo was good for three months. Until one day, there was a big event in our hometown. We were walking down the street. He always walked behind me because he never wanted any guy looking at my butt. Suddenly, someone rode by and blew the horn. Jealous, Jo thought they were blowing the horn at me. The next thing I felt was a hard punch in the back of my head. He did not know that I had a blade in my bra. I turned around so fast and started cutting him up. I guess I must have snapped. I was told I was like another person. I did not even remember anything. When I came to my realization, the police were everywhere. It was a good thing he did not like the police. He would not tell who did it. I did not realize how that messed him up. Jo had to have surgery on his hand, and he could not use his hand for five months.

That's when I began to sell drugs, making his moves, making his plays. One night, I had to bag up cocaine. I heard a voice. The voice of the enemy said, "Try it; try it." So, I put the line of powder down, but God took me back to what my mother told me and the vision I saw of my mother when she tried Coke. All I could see was the blood coming from my mother's nose and how it affected me as a child. At that time, I did not want my child to ever feel the way I felt when I saw my mother like that.

BUT GOD

From that moment on, I was grateful that my mother told me the truth, because sometimes in life our past will come only to help us with our future. Even though it may hurt and you do not understand it, eventually it turns out to be for your good.

Chapter 11

He Was Better

Jo's hand got better, and we were getting along. We were making big money selling drugs. We were taking trips, and we were getting high. Everything was working in our favor at that time. Until one day, Jo got jealous again. This time was different. He pulled out a gun on me. At that moment, I put in my mind and in my heart that I was going to kill him before he killed me. Jo finally left and came back late that night. We started fighting again. At that point, I was tired of fighting. I prayed to God and asked him to please help me get out of that situation. I got in the bed, and Jo came back with the bullshit again. Jo walked in the hallway, and suddenly I ran into the room in fear, shaking. He was holding me so tight. His exact words were, "I will never put my hands on you again."

The look on Jo's face was fear. He proceeded to tell me, "Meka, I saw your brother Reuben standing in the bathroom looking at me, clear as day." My brother Reuben died in 2001. From that day forward, Jo never hit me again.

BUT GOD

Chapter 12

Making Moves

After Jo saw my brother, he and I were making so many moves it was crazy. By *making moves,* I mean moving drugs. We were booming. Everyone was coming out of everywhere buying. There was so much money to be made. We gave each other the nickname "Bonnie and Clyde." I could remember in the early 2000's trying the "X" pills with Jo. I always dressed up in high heel shoes. That day, Jo invited me to a cookout at his mother's house. We were outside when Jo gave me the pill. I took it while sitting down. His mother told us the food was ready. As I stood up, the pill had me feeling like I was as tall as the trees. I was tripping so bad. I was high. I ducked to walk into his mother's front door. At this point, Jo noticed I was high. He said, "Man, let's go. You are tripping, ducking down." We left, and we were up all-night having sex until the next day around 3:00 p.m.

Jo said he had to make a move. So, we made a move out of town. As soon as we did a drop, we went to the mall. When I stepped out of the car, I began to get sick. I had in my mind that I must be pregnant. Jo proceeded to take me to the store to get a pregnancy test. Of course, it was positive. When I found out I was pregnant, I did not make many moves. However, I rode with Jo to make moves from time to time. One night, Jo went to make a move by himself, and I stayed

BUT GOD

home. About forty-five minutes later, Jo called my phone in a panic stating four police were chasing him.

Jo told me to meet him at a certain location. He was going to jump out so that I could pick him up. He told me to hurry up and move. I did what he told me. As soon as I got to the location, I saw him standing in the woods with a light. I went to get him, and we were on the run from the police.

One night, we were in New York sleeping at a hotel. Jo woke me up and asked me if I peed in the bed. He pulled the covers back and the bed was full of blood. He told me to go to the hospital because I was pregnant. Remember, we were on the run. I went to the bathroom instead and got a roll of tissues, and put it in my panties. But the blood would not stop. Across from the hotel was a Huddle House. I could not call the ambulance because Jo was on the run.

As soon as I went to the Huddle House, I saw a couple sitting by the door. I told them I was pregnant and bleeding. I begged them to take me to the hospital. The couple did not hesitate. The husband picked me up and took me to the truck. His wife got in the backseat with me. When we got to the hospital, they wanted to stay with me. I lied and told them someone was with me. I knew that Jo was on the run. I went in the back with the doctor, and he informed me that I lost the baby. I was so angry, because I knew the issue came from stress and being on the run with Jo. I called Jo and told him the situation. He was so upset. He said I am coming to get you. I asked him "How?"

Three hours later, I was lying in the hospital bed, and someone walked in. I heard heels coming towards me. As soon as I looked up, I busted out laughing. Jo was in a wig and dressed in high heels. He was already six foot one inches tall with big feet. He was so skinny and had on a brown dress that

BUT GOD

came to his knees. Jo put me in a wheelchair. We left the hospital. The people thought I was crying because I lost my baby. I was crying because of what Jo had on. As soon as we got in the car, he threw the heels at the car. From that day on, he dressed like a woman.

BUT GOD

Chapter 13

Still on the Run

I will never forget, and as I am writing, I am laughing now. One day I was at my grandmother's house. Jo had to manage some business, and he did not want me to go. I was sitting there waiting for him. He never told me what time he was returning. My grandma came in the room and began to whisper to me, "Someone is at the front door for you. They look like a man, but they are dressed like a woman." I laughed so hard. After all these years, I never told her it was Jo. My grandmother's house was the place I always went to get away whenever Jo made his dangerous moves.

One day, I decided to take a shower at my grandmother's house. Not knowing that Steven (from Chapter One) was in the other room. I was in the bathroom getting undressed and preparing for the shower. Once I was in the shower, I heard a voice from God saying, "Look up?" As soon as I looked up towards the shower head, you will never guess what I saw. I saw two eyeballs looking at me over the shower head. He had drilled two holes by the shower head just so that he could look at whoever was taking a shower. It was like a scary movie. I cried out in a loud voice to my daddy in fear. I jumped out of the shower in fear. Still in shock, I said "Daddy, take me home NOW."

BUT GOD

As I was walking out of the door, Steven said, "Meka, I am going to cover those holes up." At that moment, as soon as he said those words, I knew he had a serious problem. I told Daddy, and he begged me not to because he knew Jo would kill him. Daddy told me to go to the police instead, then he dropped me off at home. An hour later, I got a call from Daddy. He had discovered that Steven had eight holes in the bathroom, in the mirror, through the wall, and in the floor so that he could see someone using the bathroom, one from outside the bathroom to see your backside, and some others. Daddy was so mad.

As I was driving to the police station the next day, it felt like a movie God replayed in my mind. God took me back to the age of six when Steven first molested me. Images of the same two adults who told me not to tell when I was six flooded my mind, but I was finally an adult. I faced those same two adults to tell them I was going to report Steven. They could not stop me then, since I was an adult. They have hated me ever since. I really felt if they had not put fear in me at the age of six, Steven would not have done all the things he did.

Chapter 14

Look at God

God works in mysterious ways. God will always show up and show out for His chosen ones. One day, I spent some time at my grandmother's house while Jo handled some business. Around 10:00 p.m., I was watching television, and I had just smoked some good weed. I fell asleep on the sofa. I began to fall into a deep sleep. I had a dream, but I could not remember what it was about. The only thing I remember was I jumped off the sofa and saw Steven jumping up off the floor. I thought I was dreaming because when I went to sleep, the only person who was there was my grandmother. Steven was sick in the head. What I saw blew my mind, and it made me so angry. Steven jumped up and walked into the back room. There were some kids lying on the floor, covering their bottom parts. It took me back to the time I was six years old. I began to think. "HELL NO! He did not do what I thought he did to those kids?" I pulled the covers off the kids and their panties were down. I asked the same questions I asked when I was six years old. I asked them did somebody touch you all, and the kids said, "YES!"

I already knew what the bastard did because he did the same thing to me. I just wanted them to confirm it. At that point, I told the kids to get up and I called their mommas immediately. My grandmother came out the room yelling, "Put that phone down. You are trying to start some mess." I looked my grandmother in the eyes. "If you wouldn't have told me not to tell at the age of six, this would not be happening to them at the ages of six, five, and three!" I told her, "You stopped me then, but you cannot stop me now. I am going to the police with this." She held her chest like she was having a heart attack, but I did not believe that.

The police came right away. They put handcuffs on Steven. At that moment, I returned to that six-year-old child. Finally, I got justice for myself. God reminded me that what happened in my past made me stronger for my future. I broke a generational curse. From that day on, my grandmother and my aunt acted funny towards me. You can ask me if I care, and I will tell you, "No." I saved those kids from being molested like I was molested. Now, I do not go to my grandmother's house. The love from her is not there because I exposed what Steven had been doing. God gets all the glory for allowing me to be in the right place at the right time. Now justice has been served. During all of this, Jo and I finally split up.

Chapter 15

My Second Relationship

One day I decided to go for a walk around town. It was a beautiful summer day in 2005. I had on a sexy outfit on, and I always walked in high heels. So many people used to ask me how I did not know the person.

Weeks later, a person came by my home and asked me, "Did someone in a grey Chevy ask you if you wanted a ride?" At that moment, I knew exactly who he was talking about. I thought the guy was so ugly. As time passed, the guy, in the car, Tom, started to hang out with the person that I knew. One day, he started asking if he could have my number. I always said "no" and to tell the guy he was so ugly. But after some time, I finally gave him my number.

Tom and I talked on the phone. The conversation was good, and we became good friends. I really did not know he was older than me because he did not look like it. Three months later, we did not have sex, but just lots of fun. A year later, I felt myself liking him, but I did not tell him. One day, Tom asked me if I wanted to go to the beach. Of course, I said "Yes." When he took his shirt off, my heart melted. He was so fine under his shirt. I used to say if I could take his face and put it somewhere else, I would go with him. Tom was very romantic. We had a wonderful time.

BUT GOD

It is crazy how Tom finally asked me if I would be his lady. I explained to him that I loved my single life, and I was not bullshitting. We decided to become a couple. The fourth year came, and I was pregnant with my second child, a baby boy. Tom was such a good provider. He told me I did not have to work. I stayed home while he worked out of town. He always returned to check on me and treated me like a queen. I walked in such high heels. That was my thing. On this day, as I was walking, I saw a grey box Chevy on twenty-four-inch rims. Passing by at first, the driver made a U-turn in the road and asked me if I wanted a ride. Of course, I said, "No."

Chapter 16

The Bullshit

The Lord started giving me dreams about Tom and another woman. I would ask Tom and he would always deny it. I told Tom, "I don't dream for nothing, and I keep having the same dream." One day I got a restricted call from a lady asking me if I knew Tom. I told her, "Yes, we have been together for almost five years." She told me that she and Tom had just gotten married. At that moment, I called Tom and asked him, but he kept denying it. He said he was on his way home. I was going off on him. I was pregnant, and he just got married. He came home crying. He finally said, "I am going to tell you the truth." I told him. "Look nigger, I told you from the start, I do not have time for bullshit, and I love my single life. You played a game on me. If I were not pregnant, I would do you in." So, he sat me down on the bed and said, "Let me tell you a story."

He said he was dealing with this woman for years before he met me, and they had kids together. The story he told me sounded like a lie. But he told me he went to see the kids and when he got there, the lady already had the rings. They went to the courthouse and got married. I was like, "Nigger who do you think you running a game on So, she put a gun to your head and made you go to the courthouse?" As a woman, I have a heart for other women. I felt bad because he had me drive up there and he divorced her the same day. He told me,

BUT GOD

"Meka, I will do anything to be with you." I explained to him, "The bullshit you did to that woman and me, is going to come back to you."

The lady came to town and standing outside (where) in the rain. She was screaming and crying asking him why. Tom told her, "I am done. I am in love with Meka and that is that."

Chapter 17

After the Baby

After the baby was born, Tom was a wonderful father. He had a lot to prove because he already knew I was going to get him back. He would take me on shopping sprees and give me money. He did everything, acting out of the norm. I took Tom through hell. I already had hate in my heart for men anyway, so it was easy to take him through hell. I wanted him to hurt a thousand times worse than I did. I could remember getting a babysitter and staying out all weekend with another man, having sex videos and sending them to Tom's phone. I wanted to make sure he knew I was with someone else. I was showing the guy's face and everything.

    As time passed, I told Tom I needed some space. I was lying in the bed with another man. I had a feeling someone was looking at me. My friend guy left. As soon as he left, Tom walked out of the closet. Tom had broken into my house and hid in my closet. When he walked out of the closet, he said, "If I had my gun, I would have shot both of y'all." We started to fight. I had a blade under my pillow, and I started cutting him all over and did not care. While I was cutting him, I was yelling, "Nigger you tried me. You went and got married and now I got a second child." Blood was everywhere. Tom started passing out. I had to take him to the hospital. I whispered in his ear, "If you tell them I did it, I am leaving you." He told the hospital staff he got in a fight at the club.

Chapter 18

Year Six

Time flew by, and Tom and I were doing the same old bullshit off and on thing. One day, we decided to get things together. Tom and I moved to a different location, and things began to go right for us for about seven months. God started to show me dreams once again. I told Tom like I said before, "I don't dream for nothing, so what is going on?" He denied it. I kept having dreams of a big, python snake hanging over the door of the bathroom. I knew it was the enemy close to us. I really did not understand the vision at that time.

One day, I fell asleep, and God gave me a vision of Tom and someone close to me having sex in my bed. I had this dream three times, so I knew there was something behind it. The person in the dream, I would not believe it was her, because we were so close. I asked Tom many times, and he denied it. Shay Shay was a close cousin of mine. When I ate, she ate. When I was drunk, she got drunk. I took care of her as a child. But I worked from six to two at McDonald's. I used to leave Shay Shay home while I went to work. She would be home waiting for me to get ready to smoke because I sold weed back then. When I walked in the door, we would laugh and have a fun time like the old days.

BUT GOD

Chapter 19

Betrayal

I am so blessed that God blessed me with a gift. No matter what people or strangers try to do to me, God always reveals it to me. One day, Shay Shay and I were sitting on the couch. She said, "Let us call a psychic." So, we did. The call was on the speaker phone, and she spoke to the psychic first. When it was my time to speak to the psychic, the first thing the psychic said was, "I see you be around a person, and she is a snake." It blew my mind. As soon as she heard the psychic say that she burst into tears. Shay Shay said out of her mouth, "I am that snake." At that very moment, God took me back to the vision of the snake hanging in my bathroom. I knew in my heart, the vision of Tom having sex in a bed with a woman was Shay Shay. I asked her why she was crying, and she never told me.

    I decided to confront Tom and asked him once again about the vision that I had, but of course he denied it. Weeks passed. Shay Shay called me and told me she saw Tom with another woman. At that time, Tom said, "I know Shay Shay isn't talking?" I told my oldest sister Shay Shay and Tom had sex in my bed. I told her to ask her because she would not tell me. Shay Shay told my sister, "YES." I got in my car and went to Shay Shay's house. Her mom was there. I asked her mom was Shay Shay there. Her mom said she was in the back room. When Shay Shay saw me walk through her room door, her eyes got as big as marbles. I spit in her face and walked out. I went to Tom's job and busted all his car windows and flattened all his tires.

Of course, Tom denied it, but I wanted to fuck someone that was close to him to get him back. I did just that. Of course, I made a video for him to see. He was hurt, but I felt good. Once again, that hate towards a man was there, and it was raging more. I felt I let my guard down. This was the second time this man tried me. After this incident, we took a break from each other for two months, but I let him come back again.

Chapter 20

Shay Shay

God started showing me visions of Shay Shay killing herself. I was too mad at her to reach out to her. I felt like nothing or no one should have come between us. I kept ignoring the dreams about her until one day I heard God say, "Forgive Shay Shay," because I had forgiven Tom. One day, I decided to go to Shay Shay's mom's house. I asked her mom where she was. As I was walking to Shay Shay's room, God said, "Just open the door." She was writing a suicide letter. This was eight months after the situation with Tom happened. Shay Shay said she was about to kill herself because she could not handle this issue. She had a gun under her pillow.

My God sent me there to forgive her. By me listening to God's voice, it saved her life. We held each other and cried. I asked her when she slept with Tom. She said, "Do you remember when Tom brought you those dozens of roses when you got off work? That was the happiest day of your life, but that was the worst day of my life." I did not know he had just fucked my friend before he brought me the flowers.

BUT GOD

Chapter 21

I Am TIRED

After that, I was wondering what was next. Tom was acting so nice. I knew it had to be something. For some reason, Tom kept telling me, "You will never leave me." I really wanted to leave Tom, but for some strange reason, I could not leave. Tom and I were always breaking up, fighting, and then getting back together. It was getting old. I can remember one day, Tom and I got into a big fight. I hit him in the face with a candle. Do you know he kicked me so hard that he kicked my teeth to the back of my mouth? I was on the floor.

In my mind, I was thinking, it is on! I had on leggings and Tom wanted to have oral sex after he realized what he had done. Little did Tom know, I was about to FUCK him up. Tom took all my clothes off and started rubbing on me. I told Tom to turn around so that I could massage his back. He turned around. I picked up my leggings and wrapped them around Tom's neck, choking him. He was throwing up and coughing out of anger until someone knocked at the door. That is the only reason Tom is alive today.

I began to tell my mom I was no longer happy with Tom. I was living with Tom. My mom said, "Meka, if you are not happy, you have to move on." I told my mom, "I cannot, but I do not know why."

BUT GOD

God started to show me a dream. I was dreaming of a white nurse. In the dream, the nurse had a black penis instead of a vagina and she was walking towards me. I did not understand the dream at that time. God showed me the dream for a second time. I went to my grandmother who was a preacher and explained to her the dream that I was having. My grandmother explained to me that it sounded like witchcraft.

Grandma explained the roots to me. She said that Tom was tying something to his penis, and every time we had sex, he was inserting it inside of me. My grandmother prayed for me. Weeks passed, and I went to the restroom squatting. God said "Look." I was in shock. As I was looking, I saw a black string hanging out of my virga. I started to pull it out. It was two to three inches long. I admittedly called my grandmother. She told me to not have sex with Tom, and I did not for a long while. Tom began to wonder why we were not having sex. I told him I knew about the roots, and he laughed it off.

Chapter 22

I Remember!

I remember that I was so tired of being in a relationship with Tom. I had sex with someone who I was cheating on him with. I told him to put two hickeys on my neck. The guy did not know what I was up to. One morning, Tom was dropping me off for work. We were driving down highway 301. Tom told me he wanted to have sex when he got off work. My words to him were, "I am good. I already had sex." I showed him the hickeys on my neck and slammed the door.

When it was time to get off work, I saw a yellow Cutlass coming my way. I already knew it was about to be a big fight. By then, I did not care.

I entered the car. He was playing the song, "The Devil Made Me Do It." I was thinking in my head, "Oh shit, he plays this song." It was about to be some crazy shit going on. We were riding down the road, and Tom pulled out a knife and stabbed me in the knee. I grabbed the knife while he was driving, and the car was going from side to side. He knew once I got the knife, I was going to stab him. That is exactly what I did. Both of us ended up in the emergency room. I stabbed him in the side, and his side started to swell up. We both lied and said somebody attacked us, but we did not know who it was.

BUT GOD

We both agreed we needed a break from each other. This time, we broke up for two months.

Chapter 23

What the Hell?

Two months passed, and I did not know I was pregnant again by Tom. I was wondering what I was going to do. I called him and explained to him that I was pregnant. He was so excited because we had not been talking. We ended up back together because I did not want to go through the pregnancy alone. I already had two boys, and I wanted a girl. Tom and I decided to have a gender reveal party. Just my luck, I found out I was having a baby girl. I was getting bigger, and I was 20 weeks and five days exactly. Normally, my sister went with me to the doctor because Tom worked out of town. Finally, I was 24 weeks, and I had a 3-D ultrasound. My sister was supposed to go with me, but she was not able to. I ended up going alone.

The doctor gave me a glucose drink for a test, and I waited an hour in the waiting room. The nurse called me back to the room and laid me on the examination table. During the ultrasound, the nurse looked at me very strangely. I asked her "What?" All she said was, "Did someone come with you?" I told her "NO!" and asked "WHY?" She did not answer me. Then, she said she could not find the baby's heartbeat. She repeated it. Immediately, I saw the cross that I used to see a while back. God gave me peace. I asked her, "What are you saying? Is my baby dead?" She said, "Let me get the Doctor."

BUT GOD

Chapter 24

The Unbelief

The doctor entered the room, and she began to examine me, trying to find the baby's heartbeat. She looked at me with tears in her eyes and said, "I cannot find the baby's heartbeat." The morning of the glucose test, I had to drink the liquid to prepare for the test, and my baby was moving fine. I told the doctor it had to be the drink because my baby was moving fine. By then, I was confused and mad. But I still saw the cross, so I knew God was there with me.

The doctor explained to me I would have to keep the child in my stomach for two more weeks because my body was still thinking I was pregnant. If she were to put me into labor, I could bleed to death. All I could do at that point was talk to God, because I knew he was there. I told God he would have to be with me through this walk. I walked out of the doctor's office six months pregnant. I called Tom and my family and told them the situation. They were confused about what the doctor said.

As I drove home, God said, "Do not worry. I am going to give you your baby girl." I went home and fell asleep. God gave me a vision of me having a baby girl. I had a choice. I could either lay down and be depressed or get up, live, and praise God. I decided to get up, live, and praise GOD. My family would look at me crazy and confused because I was living like nothing was going on. I would still go to the store, pump gas, cook, and live normally. So many people would ask me when I was due, and I would just say, "Soon."

I can remember one night, my faith was so strong in God that when I laid down, I could feel something moving. I thought God was working a miracle. I returned to the hospital and told them the situation and asked if they could check me again. They explained to me that people die and still move inside body bags. I kept my faith in God because He told me I would have a baby girl.

Chapter 25

The Day of the Delivery

The day of the delivery, I was so glad to get the baby out of my stomach. I named the baby Shabria. She would have been eight years old today. The day of the delivery there were so many of my family members there to support me. It was my best friend and me in the room, and they put me into labor. The contractions began to kick in. I was in so much pain. All I could do was keep in my mind that God was with me. Everyone kept asking me if I were okay, but I kept comforting them. My best friend walked out of the room for five minutes. I felt the baby coming out. I called for the nurses, and they came running. The baby was delivered. They asked me to hold her. I said, "No." I did not even want to look at her, and I did not. But Tom held her, and he cried. I found myself comforting him as well. I could hear God telling me "Peace." It was at that moment that I knew that my living baby girl was on the way. Three months after that, I broke up with Tom after twelve years.

BUT GOD

Chapter 26

A New Beginning

It was six months after Shabria's death that I finally looked at her pictures. She was so beautiful with a head full of hair and beautiful little lips. Even though she was an angel now, I was so glad she did not look like Tom. As time passed, I kept standing on God's promise, and I kept living my life being single. Blessings just started falling out of the sky as soon as I left Tom. It was like *WOW*. It is funny how you think you could be in love with someone and they can hinder you from what God has for you in life.

After two years passed, I met a guy and got pregnant. We were not together, but we had an understanding. Guess what? God did just want he said he was going to do. I know I was not married, but it was time for me to go to the doctor to see what I was having. Guess what? The doctors said it was a girl. All I said was "Thank you, JESUS." Of course, the enemy tried to come in my ear and say, "You are going to lose this baby, too." But I will always hear God's voice say, "Fear not. I blessed you with this baby. You are going to have this baby. All is well." I went the entire term, and I was blessed with a healthy baby girl who weighed nine pounds and six ounces. I named her Journee because it was a journey before her. I had her through a C-section.

When I walked down the hallway, guess what? The same doctor that I had years ago, who knew in the heart that it was something they did, was walking my way. She was looking puzzled and said, "Shameka." I looked into her eyes and my words were, "I forgive you because I had hate in my heart for you. Look at God. He blessed me with another baby girl." The doctor cried and held my hand because she knew, but she never said a word out of her mouth. But before she walked away, she said, "Thank you for forgiving me."

Chapter 27

Still Attached

Journee's father and I had an understanding. It got to the point that he wanted to marry me. I explained to him that I had just gotten out of a relationship, and I needed some time to be single. He was a great father and a good provider. I worked during the day, and I needed a babysitter. He kept Journee for me at my house. Journee's father brought me some balloons, and the helium began to seep out. This day, Journee's father called me on the phone while I was working. He said he was scared. He explained to me he heard little footsteps running down the hall. At that time, Journee could not even walk. I had a dog named "Baby," and he would bark at the balloons. He went to look down the hallway, and he saw the balloons moving by themselves as the dog was barking at them. I did not believe it until he called me on Facetime to show me. I knew at that time it was Shabria who had passed away.

    I started to explain to Journee's father that I would dream about her all the time after her passing. I remember one night I was lying in bed. My bed was extremely high, and I had sheets with skirting on them. As I was dozing off, it scared me. I felt a baby climbing to get in the bed with me. I explained to my grandma that I kept having spirits visit. Grandma explained to me that I had to say her name aloud and let her know that it was okay for her to pass to the other side. This was necessary to release her. As soon as I did that, I did not dream about Shabria anymore.

As Journee grew older, I would hear her talking to someone I couldn't see. I never told her about her sister. I asked her one day, "Who are you talking to in the room?" She said, "My sister." Journee would be playing and talking, having a good time. I just accepted it and let it be.

Chapter 28
My Life Changed

My life changed in a major way for the good. As I think back over my past life, I was very quick-tempered. I used to go from zero to one thousand at any point. I never really bothered anyone. The most important thing was I had a relationship with God.

One day while I was sleeping, God gave me a vision of two guys getting into an argument. In the dream as the guys were arguing, my best friend got shot. The vision was so real that I jumped up at 3:00 a.m. and called him to make sure it was not real. Two weeks later, I was home, and I received a phone call from a female saying, "Come pick me up." Instead of two guys, it was two women fighting. I was placed in a situation in real life with someone close to me who was in a toxic relationship. I witnessed naturally the same exact thing that was in my dream.

Let me tell you about God. God allowed me to experience those feelings in the vision for a reason. God was preparing my mind, because he knew what was coming down the road in the natural. I witnessed someone's life being taken right in front of my eyes, but I could not react. All I could do was praise God and thank him for covering my mind because He prepared me for what was happening at that moment. What

I can tell everyone who reads this book is I screamed to my friend Sarah, "Don't do it!" It was not Sarah; it was a demonic spirit that took control over her. As I was yelling her name, she did not even hear me. It was like an out of body experience. We were in a very rural area where there were cows and all types of noises around us on Highway 301. It was a busy highway. But when the homicide happened, it was complete silence. You could hear pin drop. It was an out of body experience. After it happened, I saw the demonic spirit jump out of her and her face turned back to her regular image. All Sarah said was, "What have I done?"

From that moment on, I realized that God allowed me to see this to change my ways. Because I saw that, my life totally changed. Now I think before I react, and I try to stay out of harm's way.

Chapter 29

The Turn Around

After I witnessed someone's life being taken, I now separate myself from situations and people who I know will come into my life and cause drama. I do not like to get mad. Sometimes, I have flashbacks of seeing the demonic spirit on Sarah's face. When I see that vision, I can calm myself down and let it go. I have four kids to raise and a family to take care of. I refuse to let the devil use my mind to take my life from my kids. My message to everyone today is, it is okay to walk away from someone you love or from a situation that hurts you heart. Hurt can turn into anger. Anger can turn into violence, and in the end, someone can end up dead or in jail.

BUT GOD

Chapter 30
God Is ALIVE

As I continued to reflect over my life, I will always say, "Thank you, Jesus." He has never left me or forsaken me. Like God said, *"I knew you before you were in your mother's womb,"* **Jeremiah 1:5**. To me, that verse means God already knows the beginning and the end of our lives. He knows the flesh on this earth, and it is up to us to trust God in any storm that comes into our lives. Starting at the age of six and not understanding the meaning of GOD, he showed me with a sign in the image of a cross. He showed me in a cross so that I can have a better understanding. God's love flows so much from the spirit realm, and it is such an amazing feeling. The most impressive thing about GOD is I was the only one who could see it. I felt the embrace of the Almighty's arms of love around me. The feeling flowed with me until I got older and began to understand and have a relationship with him. Now that I am older, I can think back over it. I was different from everyone else in my family. It is amazing. Now, I can say I accept the calling that is on my life. Why? Because I am chosen. I am bold. And I am not ashamed of GOD. He is **ALIVE**.

BUT GOD

Chapter 31

But GOD

I am so grateful that God always kept His hands on me. Even during that time, I was not praying. Even when I was in the streets and doing whatever I wanted to do, God kept his loving arms around me. All the things I went through in my past, I could have grown up to be a lesbian. Why? Because I was raped at an early age. I have friends who were being raped as well. I had to witness my sister being raped. I had to save multiple family members from being raped. Also, my grandmother liked women because she was raped as a child. But God had his hands on me through all that I endured. God did that because He knew he had a better plan for me. I am not going to lie, all that trauma caused hate in my heart towards men. God had to deliver me, and He is still working on me by healing me from my past hurt, even on today. All that did was make a strong queen.

I am not desperate for a man or seeking love from a man. God blessed me with a loving father and a mother. My parents made sure I felt love, and they told me daily that they loved me. So, with the love from God, my parents, and the love I have for myself gave me the boldness and courage to know that I am loved.

BUT GOD

Chapter 32

GOD Did It!

When I look back over my life, I realized I could have been in prison many times. From selling drugs, stabbing my ex-boyfriend, fighting, and so much more, God protected me. He kept His hands on me in the midst of my mess. Now that I am older, I realize I have work to do for God. All the things I went through were building my testimony. My testimony is to share with the world that no matter what you go through in life, God is the captain of your life. You may fall or jump off the boat, but God is the water, the sun, and the air. God is the author of life. God will always have the last say so over your life. We just must trust God and seek for understanding. We must know that all things work together for our good no matter how things look **(Matthew 6:33).** Just trust GOD. I understand it may not always be easy, but keep your faith in GOD. Do not doubt in your heart. Know that God can make the impossible, possible. He can do just what He said he will do. My message to everyone is simple, "Do not give up on God, because he will never give up on you."

BUT GOD

Chapter 33

Now Faith

People, FAITH is the key to life. You must know without a doubt that God is going to move in your life. No matter what the situation is or what you went through in your life, just know better days are coming. How do I know? I am a living witness. I know many people who have been through past trauma in their lives. Maybe they have chosen drugs or they are involved in prostitution or alcohol, but they do these things to try to block out the trauma that took place in their lives. Some people are gay because they have been raped. It is so sad to see that because I went through similar things. I am often asked why I am not on drugs or involved with the same sex. I explain that it is not by my own strength or my own might. It is God's hand on my life and the blood of Jesus over my mind to not allow my past to dictate my future or my emotions. The key is to have a relationship with God and always keep my faith in Him. When the enemy tries to bring up your past, you must replace that thought with something good. If I could look in your eyes, I would tell you, "If God did it for me, He will do for you."

To everyone who is reading this book, please just let go of any past hurt or trauma. Give it to God. If it has been hunting you for years, I know everyone is different and I am not saying it is easy. Just put it in your heart, put it in your mind and speak it out of your mouth, "God, I give it to you," and you must leave it there. Trust me, I had to do the same thing years ago. If you do that, you will feel peaceful like never before. We must understand that the battle starts in our minds. You must put a shield over your mind. That shield is the blood of Jesus. With the blood of Jesus, the enemy cannot enter your thoughts. People, I am telling you the truth. You must command your mind, will and emotions to submit to the obedience to Christ in you. Then, you will see the change. If you must do this daily, do it. I am telling you it works. I hope my book touches someone's life in a major way. I pray you get understanding, wisdom and knowledge. I pray you know God is with you at the beginning of your life, middle, day, night, and at the end. God is with you always. He is love.

Acknowledgments

I wanted to thank everyone who played a big part in helping me get my first book published. I'm so grateful that God sent the right people on my path to reach amazing goals in my life. May God bless each and all of you. I wish blessings upon you all. Thanks again.

BUT GOD

About the Author

Shameka Hatcher lives in a small town in Georgia. She is a woman because God has shown her time after time to just have faith the size of a mustard seed. He will do the impossible. Shameka is grateful for her relationship with God. She describes the feeling as amazing, as well as the peace and joy that come from GOD!! Neither her past nor anyone can take that away from her!! She is a queen, and she is bold and fearless. Why? Because she has been chosen from the Most High.

Contacting the Author

Email: shamekahatcher5@gmail.com

Made in the USA
Middletown, DE
04 April 2024